Gooseberry Patch ®

the Country Friends ®
Collection

Gift Baskets

Mary Elizabeth
... gives cookie sacks to all her neighbors at Christmas.

Kate
...thinks every gift basket should contain chocolate.

Holly
... packs bath gels & lotions for wonderful relaxation baskets.

Save your

Cans

...all shapes & sizes can be painted, decorated & disguised as clever containers!

Hand-paint a design or use a stencil on a spray-painted can.

Wrap a can with strips of fabric or ribbon.

Crackle-finish a can!

Glue on a wooden cutout, or a decoration made of craft foam sheets.

Poke holes in a can & thread a wire through 'em for a handle ... then glue on a copy of this label for an easy container!

I'm so glad we're Friends.

Spectacular Sacks

... take a plain old paper bag & turn it into something special!

Sew on a fabric star or heart or ...whatever!

↳ Cut out a design and then back the "hole" with fabric or pretty paper.

Glue on a pair of ribbons and use 'em to tie your bag shut. ↗

Cut slits around top of sack ⌐ thread ribbon through slits & tie a bow in front.

Handpaint a design on the bag, fold over to close ... and sew a button on to keep it shut!

Copy this label & glue it on a sack full o' homemade cookies!

THE ONLY WAY TO GET RID OF A TEMPTATION IS TO YIELD TO IT.
— OSCAR WILDE —

Enjoy!

Hmmm... *handsome*

Holders... containers..
cute

No matter whatcha call 'em, don't forget that the presentation is half the fun of the present!

Jars

can be easily recycled into terrific gift containers.

Cut a fabric circle and top a Mason jar with it, securing it in place with ribbon, raffia or even good old twine. You can fill it with homemade goodies, potpourri or store-bought candies.

Kate's

★ Iced Jars

... so simple!

Begin with a clean clear jar, any size. Just draw a design on the outside of the jar with fingernail polish ✓ any color or clear. Now just sprinkle the wet polish with plain old table salt or glitter. Let dry, then use as a sparkling gift jar for a candle or any little favor...

you are just ☆ TOO ☆ *clever!*

★ A fun idea ! Remember those old-time wire milk bottle carriers? Find enough old bottles or jars to fill it... and fill each bottle with a different colorful hard candy! Carry it off to your favorite friend-with-a-sweet-tooth.

♥ You're Sweet ♥

FOR YOU

ravishing receptacles... *creative* caddies....

Hunt for the perfect container. Think of the recipient.
Be imaginative! Have fun!

> "There's a better way to do it. Find it!" ~ THOMAS EDISON

TURN A FANCY FLEA MARKET HAT UPSIDE DOWN & FILL IT WITH A TEA PARTY FOR ONE :

* Pretty china cup & saucer
* Teabags
* Flavored sugars
* Collectable silver spoon
* Tin of gourmet lemon drops
* A lacy napkin
* Old gloves

FOR A BELOVED BABYSITTER, FIND A BIG BLACK SATCHEL OR EVEN A VINYL PURSE ~ SOMETHING A LA MARY POPPINS ~ AND PACK IT FULL OF SITTER'S SURVIVAL STUFF :

* Box of Designer Bandages
* A pretty notepad & pen
* A card game & activity books
* Disney video
* Small flashlight
* Headache medicine
* A book to read to the kids
* Gift certificate to her favorite shop.

EMBELLISH A PLASTIC PAIL WITH SILLY BUMPER STICKERS FOR A NEW CAR/NEW DRIVER GIFT AND FILL 'ER UP :

* sponge & car wash supplies * road maps
* driving gloves * jumper cables * key chain
* auto club membership * emergency candle
* fuzzy dice * litter bag

5

Best·O·Wishes
PARTY
B·U·C·K·E·T
...FILLED WITH EVERYTHING FOR A PERFECT PARTY

HAPPY BIRTHDA

VICKIE

One thing everybody in the world wants & needs is friendliness. —Wm Hollar

A FUN GIFT
FOR A FAVORITE
CO★WORKER!

PAINT A GALVANIZED PAIL WITH BRIGHT ENAMEL LETTERS... SPELL OUT A NAME OR A SENTIMENT... MAKE IT **BOLD**.

FILL THE BUCKET with FUN PARTY STUFF!

HORNS & WHISTLES & NOISEMAKERS

PARTY HATS

POPPERS & CONFETTI

STREAMERS

PARTY PLATES & NAPKINS

HAPPY 91ST, VICKIE

A PRINTED BANNER TO HANG (ROLL IT UP & TIE WITH A RIBBON IN THE BUCKET)

BALLOONS

IT'S MY BIRTHDAY

A BADGE OF HONOR

A CARD SIGNED BY EVERYBODY

A BOTTLE OF SPARKLING CIDER

DISPOSABLE CAMERA

PARTY MUSIC

C.D. OR TAPE

PLASTIC CHAMPAGNE GLASSES

CLOWNIN'

HEY! WHAT'S IN THERE?

* ★ RUBBER CHICKEN
* ★ BIG RED NOSE
* ★ JAR OF BUBBLES
* ★ CANNED SNAKES
* ★ WHOOPEE CUSHION
* ★ BUZZERS ★ WHISTLES
* ★ JOKE & RIDDLE BOOKS
* ★ SLAP-STICK VIDEOS — THREE STOOGES, MARX BROTHERS, JERRY LEWIS
* ★ FRIGHT WIG

...SURE TO CURE WHAT AILS YOU!

A man isn't poor if he can

AROUND

CONTAINER IDEAS:

* **A** BUCKET O' LAUGHTER
... paint a pail in bright happy polka dots!

* painted coffee can stuffed with fun!

Don't forget the
* Confetti
* Balloons
* silly glasses
* Plastic bugs

THIS BEING CRAZY IS SERIOUS BUSINESS

still L.A.U.G.H. — RAYMOND HITCHCOCK

Sweet Berry Basket

for a "berry" special friend

♥ **Sweet stuff to hide inside:**

♥ recipes & fixin's for a delicious fruit dip
♥ homemade berry jam
♥ a loaf of strawberry bread
♥ a strawberry-shaped cookie cutter
♥ berry-scented bath gel or lotion

FRUIT DIP

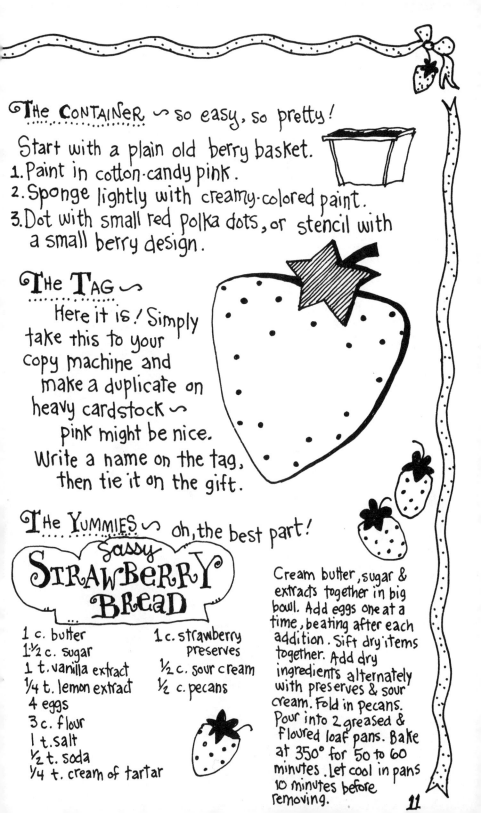

The Container ～ so easy, so pretty!

Start with a plain old berry basket.
1. Paint in cotton-candy pink.
2. Sponge lightly with creamy-colored paint.
3. Dot with small red polka dots, or stencil with a small berry design.

The Tag ～

Here it is! Simply take this to your copy machine and make a duplicate on heavy cardstock ～ pink might be nice. Write a name on the tag, then tie it on the gift.

The Yummies ～ oh, the best part!

Sassy Strawberry Bread

1 c. butter
1½ c. sugar
1 t. vanilla extract
¼ t. lemon extract
4 eggs
3 c. flour
1 t. salt
½ t. soda
¼ t. cream of tartar

1 c. strawberry preserves
½ c. sour cream
½ c. pecans

Cream butter, sugar & extracts together in big bowl. Add eggs one at a time, beating after each addition. Sift dry items together. Add dry ingredients alternately with preserves & sour cream. Fold in pecans. Pour into 2 greased & floured loaf pans. Bake at 350° for 50 to 60 minutes. Let cool in pans 10 minutes before removing.

11

FILL A GIANT POPCORN TUB OR BOWL WITH:

* GOURMET POPCORN
* POPCORN SEASONINGS
* MOVIE VIDEO
* MOVIE PASSES
* ENTERTAINMENT MAGAZINES
* NECK PILLOW
* MOVIE-STYLE CANDY LIKE JUJUBES, LICORICE, ETC.
* CANS OR BOTTLES OF SODA

Movie

Plan your gift around a favorite movie or theme!

COUNTRY FRI POPCORN

Movies are a dream world. Eat popcorn and dream. ~ SAM SHEPARD

Madness

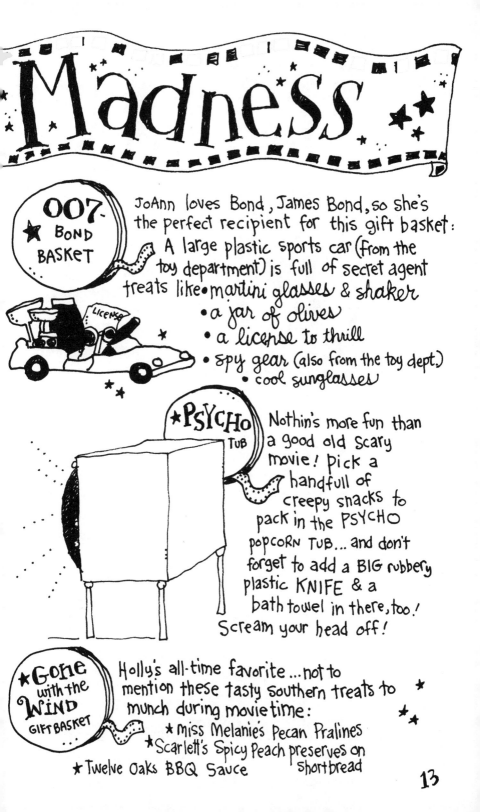

007 BOND BASKET

JoAnn loves Bond, James Bond, so she's the perfect recipient for this gift basket: A large plastic sports car (from the toy department) is full of secret agent treats like
- martini glasses & shaker
- a jar of olives
- a license to thrill
- spy gear (also from the toy dept.)
- cool sunglasses

PSYCHO TUB

Nothin's more fun than a good old scary movie! Pick a handfull of creepy snacks to pack in the PSYCHO POPCORN TUB... and don't forget to add a BIG rubbery plastic KNIFE & a bath towel in there, too! Scream your head off!

Gone with the WIND GIFT BASKET

Holly's all-time favorite...not to mention these tasty southern treats to munch during movie time:
- Miss Melanie's Pecan Pralines
- Scarlett's Spicy Peach preserves on shortbread
- Twelve Oaks BBQ Sauce

13

MOVIES

admit one to the

POPCORN POPS

... a country friends® twist on an old movie favorite!

....

4 QTS. POPPED POPCORN
(²/3 c. UNPOPPED)
1 c. PEANUTS
1 c. LIGHT MOLASSES
1 c. GRANULATED SUGAR
1 t. SALT

......

Combine popped corn & peanuts in large bowl. In a saucepan, combine molasses, sugar & salt; cook over medium heat. Pour slowly over popcorn & peanuts ~ stir until well·blended. Press into 5 oz. cold drink cups. Insert a wooden skewer in each; let cool, then peel cup away. Wrap each in plastic wrap for gift·giving.

> Every Successful creative person creates with an audience of **one** in mind.
>
> —KURT VONNEGUT

★ **Other** good movies to build a theme around:

★ Sound of Music ★ JAWS
★ Wizard of OZ
★ Pink Panther ★ BABE
★ use your imagination!

14

Movie Madness Macadamia Cheesy Puffs

...Frankly, my dear, these are delicious.

1 c. buttermilk biscuit mix
1 c. unsalted macadamia nuts, finely chopped
1 c. Gruyère cheese, shredded
½ c. butter, softened
1 egg, beaten
½ t. ground white pepper

Combine all ingredients and stir until soft dough forms. Drop by the spoonful on a greased baking sheet. Bake at 375° for 12 to 15 minutes or until very lightly browned. Cool on pan several minutes, then finish cooling on a wire rack. Store in airtight container.

FUN FILLERS

* AT PAPER SUPPLY STORES, YOU CAN USUALLY BUY POPCORN TUBS & INDIVIDUAL PAPER POPCORN BAGS TO PUT IN YOUR GIFT * ADD PAPER NAPKINS & STRAWS AS FILLERS IN YOUR MOVIE MADNESS TUB * EVEN IF YOU PUT PACKAGES OF POPCORN UNPOPPED IN YOUR GIFT, ADD SOME POPPED KERNELS TOO, JUST FOR THE FUN OF IT ~ IT WILL ALSO HELP KEEP YOUR ITEMS IN PLACE IN THE TUB * IF YOU CAN FIND SOME FILM STRIPS... PUT 'EM IN!

15

What does a COUCH POTATO need?

☐ LAP-TOP TV TRAY
☐ TV PROGRAM GUIDE
☐ UNIVERSAL REMOTE CONTROL
☐ INSULATED MUG (a big one)
☐ COUCH CADDY TO HOLD REMOTE

☐ BAKED POTATO
☐ TATER TOPPINGS
☐ BOX OF CHOCOLATES

My Life is complete.

16

Put it all together for your favorite t.v. tater.

What more could a couch potato ask for?

Give this delish recipe...

PRIMETIME POTATOES

Potatoes
Margarine
Primetime Potato Seasoning
American cheese, sliced
Bacon bits
Green onions, sliced

Slice desired number of potatoes into strips; layer in baking dish with slices of margarine. Sprinkle seasoning over layers. Bake at 350° for 30 to 45 minutes 'til tender. Completely cover taters with cheese slices. Return to oven 'til cheese melts. Top with bacon bits & green onions before serving.

... and include packets of these toppings:

PRIMETIME SEASONING -REGULAR-

3 T. dried parsley flakes
2 T. celery salt
2 T. garlic salt

- Mix & store in airtight packets.

PRIMETIME SEASONING -SPICY-

3 T. dried parsley flakes
2 T. chili powder
2 T. garlic salt
1 T. dried chives
1¼ t. celery salt
1½ t. onion powder

dash of cayenne pepper

- Mix & store in airtight packets.

For the SPORTS BUFF

...Geared for your favorite fanatic!

FILL WITH:

* Sports Blooper Video
* Sports magazines
* Universal remote control
* Team logo bumperstickers
* Sweatbands & wristbands
* Mini sports balls
* Monogrammed golf balls
* Sunblock & lip protection
* Insulated mug or water bottle
* Sports trivia encyclopedia
* Sports drinks
* Referee doll (one to tear limb from limb)
* Bags of snacks like pretzels or popcorn
* Small sports equipment, like a wastepaper basketball hoop

3 Cheers for Home Team Advantage Snack Mix

... YOU'LL SCORE BIG WITH THIS DELICIOUS PICK-ME-UP!

- 3 C. POPPED UNSALTED POPCORN
- 2 C. MINI PRETZELS
- 3 C. NACHO CHEESE-FLAVORED CHIPS
- 2·4 OZ. CANS SHOESTRING POTATO STICKS
- 1 C. PEANUTS
- ½ C. MARGARINE, MELTED
- ½ t. ITALIAN SEASONINGS
- ½ t. CHILI POWDER
- ½ t. GARLIC POWDER
- 1 T. PARSLEY FLAKES

In a large bowl, combine the first five items. Mix together melted butter & spices. Pour over snack mixture in large bowl. Toss gently until evenly coated. Spread out onto ungreased jellyroll pan. Bake at 350° uncovered for 15-20 minutes. Stir twice during cooking. Cool & store in an airtight container.

Container Ideas:

* A soft-sided beverage cooler
* Team logo trash can
* Plastic football helmet
* Baseball cap
* A tv tray
* Large lucite bowl decorated with team logos or sports memorabilia (use a decoupage medium to adhere paper items to the bowl)

Sudden Death SQUEEZE BALLS

GRAB ONE AS THE CLOCK RUNS DOWN!

* <u>heavy</u> latex balloons in team colors
  ("kid pack" balloons just don't work unless you like flour all over the place)
* flour
* funnel

1. Place balloon at end of funnel.
2. Pour flour into funnel.
3. When balloon feels squishy, tie end in knot.

PRETZELS

ADMIT ONE

STARS

REF

CHIPPOS

We are inclined to think that if we watch a football game... We have taken part in it. ~ JOHN F. KENNEDY

Sporty STUFFED SHIRTS

Begin with a t-shirt emblazoned with your sports fanatic's favorite team logo... now, with a loose running stitch, sew up the bottom of the shirt so it turns into a big "bag"... okay, you're ready to stuff the shirt with every bagged snack known to modern man! Just poke chips, pretzels, nuts, popcorn (in their bags) down the shirt neck-hole 'til it's stuffed full!

LITTLE KID'S BASKET O'BALLS

...A CLEVER GIFT FOR A JUNIOR SPORTS ENTHUSIAST.

FIND A COLORFUL PLASTIC LAUNDRY BASKET. FILL IT WITH EVERY KIND OF BALL YOU CAN FIND... basketball, football, soccer ball, plastic golf balls, rubber baseballs... GATHER A SPORTS NET OR TULLE UP AROUND IT, AND TIE IT CLOSED WITH RIBBONS.

Tape tickets to a college game or minor league event to a bottle of sports drink; drop bottle inside a team-colored-tube sock and tie shut with bright streamers.

Fisherman's Find

... a gift he won't throw back!

Container Ideas:

* A CREEL
* MINNOW BUCKET
* SMALL TACKLE BOX
* HAT WITH WIDE BRIM
* GLASS GOLDFISH BOWL
* PLASTIC BATHTUB TUGBOAT

GUIDE TO AREA LAKES

HOOKS

The most indispensable item in any fisherman's equipment is his **hat.** This ancient relic preserves not only the memory of every trout he ever caught, but also the smell.

—COREY FORD-

★ Copy this, if you wish, for a tag! Cut it out and tie it on a hat.

Fishy FILLER IDEAS:

* A BREAK-DOWN ROD
* BOOKS OR MAGAZINES ON FLY-TYING, SPORTS FISHING, AREA LAKES
* VARIOUS TACKLE including lures, hooks, spinners, bobbers
* SNACKS for NIBBLING on THE BANK~ how about FISH-SHAPED CRACKERS & GUMMY WORMS?
* SUN PROTECTION CREAMS
* FISHERMAN'S SUNGLASSES
* A TINY AQUARIUM NET (JUST FOR A GIGGLE)
* A NICE REEL & SPOOLS OF LINE
* A RULER FOR MEASURING FISH

Fill extra space with round river Pebbles & sand

GIFT CERTIFICA...

LAYER A GLASS GOLDFISH BOWL WITH LEVELS OF SAND, BOBBERS, RUBBER WORMS~ ADD A GIFT CERTIFICATE TO A FAVORITE FISHING SUPPLY SHOP ON A HOMEMADE MINIATURE BAMBOO FISHING POLE & HOOK.

God does not charge time spent FISHING against a man's allotted life span.
-American Indian proverb

Something's Afoot

... pack up a pampering pedicure, perfect for a new mom or a bride-to-be!

Container Ideas:

wire mesh basket or a soaking tub

Relax!

FOOT CREAM

FOOT MASSAGE

aaaaah!

What to Include:

- fluffy washcloths & hand towels
- pumice stone or loofah
- nail brush
- exfoliating cream
- peppermint foot lotion
- pedicure set
- massage oil
- book on reflexology
- nail polishes
- cotton footies
- satin slippers
- herbal foot soak

HOLLY'S
Herbal Foot Soak

~ INGREDIENTS ~

A handful of one herb or a combination of these, fresh or dried:

- Lavender
- Rosemary
- Sage · Comfrey

You can also add a tablespoon of Epsom Salts or baking soda. Tie up ingredients in cloth bag or washcloth and place in very warm water to steep before soaking feet.

Happiness: a way-station between too little and too much.

—CHANNING POLLOCK—

25

AM I DREAMING?

S·W·E·E·T·I·E P·I·E

Make somebody sweet a member of your own personal homemade
★ Pie of the Month Club ★
On the first of every month, deliver a scrumptious pie to your honoree:

PIE IDEAS:

- January ～ chocolate
- February ～ cherry
- March ～ maple nut
- April ～ lemon
- May ～ rhubarb custard
- June ～ strawberry
- July ～ blueberry
- August ～ peach
- September ～ apple crumb
- October ～ pumpkin
- November ～ sweet potato
- December ～ chocolate pecan

Eating well gives a spectacular JOY to life. — ELSA SCHIAPARELLI

26
58

When you deliver each pie, include the recipe.

If you're a "cake" person... adapt this idea to cakes.

pack your initial gift in a nice pie plate with:

Make miniature versions of each month's pie for singles & "dieters".

* a pie server
* pastry bags & tips
* pie divider
* ceramic pie bird
* rolling pin
* rolling pin cover
* pastry cloth
* tins of mini cookie cutters for fancy crusts
* oven mitt

MAPLE NUT PIE

★ OH ★ MY ★ IT'S GOOD

2/3 C. SUGAR
6 T. BUTTER, melted & cooled
4 EGGS
1 C. MAPLE SYRUP
1 C. WHOLE PECANS OR WALNUTS

MIX ALL INGREDIENTS TOGETHER. POUR INTO AN UNBAKED UNPREPARED PIE SHELL. BAKE AT 400° FOR 10 MINUTES. REDUCE OVEN TEMPERATURE TO 325°— BAKE ADDITIONAL 25 MINUTES 'TIL PIE IS SET & GOLDEN BROWN.

Creamy Café Au Lait

6 oz. jar non-dairy creamer
¼ c. brown sugar, packed
¼ c. decaffeinated instant coffee

Mix together all ingredients ~ store in airtight container. Be sure to include these instructions with the gift:
♥ To make one serving, mix ¼ c. of mix with ⅔ c. boiling water in mug. Stir until well blended.

Spicy Cinnamon Mocha ♥

2 c. instant cocoa mix
⅓ c. decaffeinated instant coffee
1 t. cinnamon

Mix all ingredients together ~ store in airtight container. ♥ To make one serving, mix 3 T. of mix with ⅔ c. boiling water in mug.

♥ Kate says to add some animal crackers to the gift

Sleep:
the golden chain that ties health and our bodies together.

~ THOMAS DEKKER ~

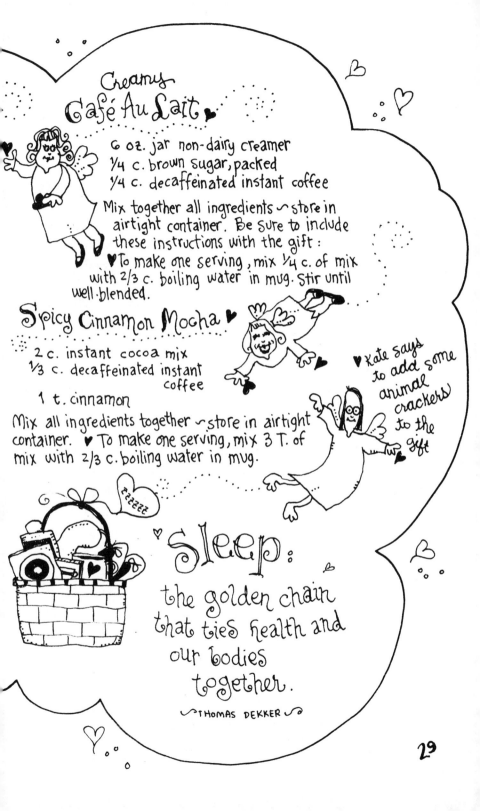

29

QUICKIES!

EASY HOUSEWARMER: Pick a mix of pretty paper napkins, one for each month or season ... stack 'em in a wicker napkin basket and tie a ribbon around the whole she·bang.

We're **OFF TO SEE THE COLLEGE** ... Stamps, postcards, prepaid phone cards, an address book with names & phone numbers, rolls of quarters, laundry soap, a mending kit, a family photo ... _whew!_ There's no limit to what an off-to-college kid needs. Pack it all in a laundry basket before you pack him off to school.

Little baby, squeeky clean, cutest thing I've ever seen!

★ Gather goodies for new baby in a plastic tub : gentle baby soaps & lotions, tiny wash cloths, a hooded towel for drying off, a rubber ducky ... and a special gift for Mom (or Dad): make a terry cloth apron for her or him to wear at splash-time!

A beginning **BAKER**, might love this: purchase a plain old apron with pockets from the craft store... use fabric paint to personalize it with a name or saying... then fill those pockets with all kinds of gadgetry: cookie cutters, rolling pin, recipe cards, oven mitts, bottles of cookie sprinkles... now fold it up carefully and put it in a basket full of homemade cookies! A great shower gift!

Holly

CHOC CHIP

I'LL SAY!

AND Speaking of Cookies...

Here's a great way to package cookies for gift-giving ⌣ easy, elegant & keeps the cookies from crumbling!

Find some clear glasses that are fairly tall, like so: (you know, the kind you sip those good, fruity, frosty drinks out of)... now, bake round cookies just a bit smaller than the glass in circumference... drop the cookies in carefully, stacking them inside the glass on top of each other 'til the glass is full. Finish it off with a wired ribbon tied around the glass vertically. → Add a sticker on the glass, over the ribbon, for a last touch... *you're ready to deliver!*

JUST ADD MILK

31

— one last idea! —

Paint a clay pot — sponge it, stripe it or gild it — and plant it full of garden goodies for a nature lover. Paper bags full of different tulips & daffodil bulbs... garden gloves, a box of bone meal, a bulb-planter... a wonderful garden gift.

I have friends in overalls whose friendship I would not swap for the favor of the kings of the world.
—THOMAS EDISON—